First published in 2007 by Timpson Limited.

ISBN 0-9547049-8-3

Timpson House Claverton Road Wythenshawe Manchester M23 9TT
Tel: 0161 946 6200 www.timpson.com
Written by John Timpson CBE. Illustrated by Robert Barrow. Printed in Great Britain.

CONTENTS

TEAM TIMPSON
TIMPSON
VIP

Why people are so important

Our people run the business

Managers can't create success on their own, they rely on their people for help, business success is a team effort. We are in the service business, that's what we sell: we don't sell things, we charge for what we do. Without the people who do those jobs, we wouldn't have a business.

We run the business

Vital Statistic

Here's a figure to make you think, 45% of the money coming through our tills is spent on employment costs, that shows how important people are to our business.

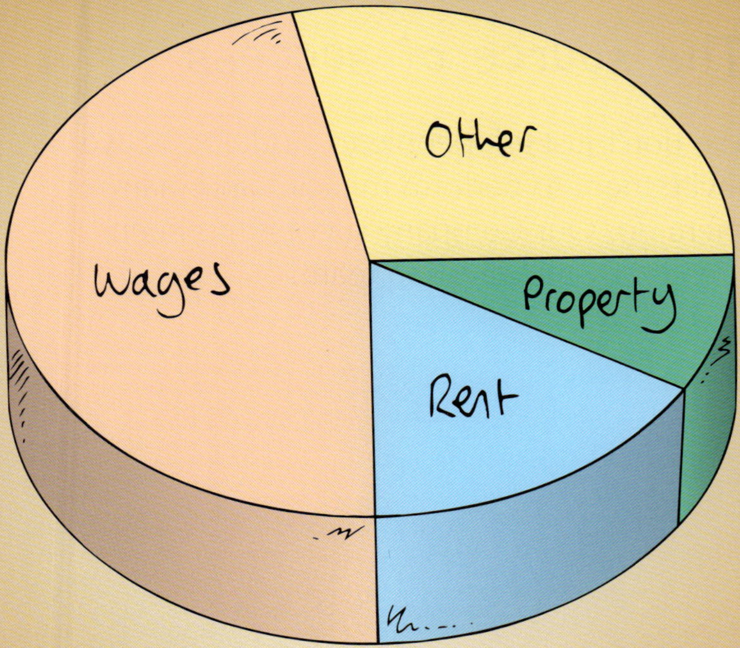

45% spent on wages

The source of success

We don't just ask people to work for us, we invite them to perform miracles and many of them do. Our Company success has been created by the Timpson team.

SALES
SERVICE
PROFIT
TIMPSON
TIMPSON
TIMPSON
People deliver results

Super Stars

Our star performers create ideas and set new standards for everyone else to follow. They continually show us how our business can get better.

Leading the business

Bonus Blockers

People with the wrong attitude stand in the way of progress. The business would be much better without them.

Drongos block progress

Pick Personalities

Businesses don't acquire the right people by luck, they get them by choice, by picking the right personalities.

Who do we need?

MR HELPFUL

MRS HAPPY

MR KEEN

MR FRIENDLY

MISS SKILLFUL

MR PUNCTUAL

MR QUICK

MR PERSONALITY

MR AMBITIOUS

MR SMART

MRS HONEST

MR FAITHFUL

Great people are easy to train...

MR SCRUFFY

MS LATE

MR IS IT FIVE 'O' CLOCK

MR RUDE

MR CARELESS

MR CAN'T DO IT

MR GRUMPY

MR DULL

MRS SLOW

MR SCROUNGER

MR DISHONEST

MISS FIB

...but these people are a nightmare

The attitude tree

People with attitude

Timpson expects everyone to have the right attitude, we don't want to work alongside Miss Lazy or Mr Grumpy. The next 4 pages show some people we like a lot.

Common sense

Look the part

Positive thinking

Self starters

Advert for diversity

Great people come in all shapes and sizes, male/female, tall/small, black/white, some become super stars.

All stars

Everyone's Welcome

We are proud that the Timpson team includes a wide range of characters from many different backgrounds. All types can be successful at Timpson, the one thing in common is the attitude they bring to work.

Proud we are inclusive

No Handicap

Many people with disabilities have created great success for Timpson. People who overcome adversity often have the determination that creates success.

Determination counts

Picture Stars

A look at a selection of our high achievers reveals the advantages of having a diverse team.

Paresh Majithia

Perry Watkins

Tricia Davies

Gouy Hamilton-Fisher

Karina Kenna

Tina Smith

Darren Brown

Glenn Edwards

Clive Stirling

Anthony Horsfield

Helen Thompson

Alex Barrett

Diversity rules

Dominant Males

We know our business does not represent the UK population. But amongst a team dominated by men, we have lots of successful women and would like to find many more.

Female superstars

No Politics

We have no time for back stabbing or selfish creeps, and have an aversion to political correctness. We like to tell it the way it is.

No nanny state

Manager

Where to find great people

Talent is available

Poor managers often complain they can't find the staff. There are plenty of good people out there but you need to know who to look for and where to find them.

The great search

Highly Recommended

Half of new Timpson employees are recommended by our own staff. The 'Introduce a Friend Scheme' is our favourite and best form of recruitment.

Introduce a friend

Work Experience

Give someone a week at Timpson and they could become employees for life. Encourage people to taste the Timpson experience. Offer work experience to sixth formers, or Christmas jobs to mature workers. We may like each other so much the situation becomes permanent.

'Timpson' experience

Customers' Recommendation

There is a new twist to our 'Introduce a Friend Scheme.' It's now available to customers as well as staff. Leaflets in our shops will not only expand our recruitment drive, but also give us a chance to tell customers why Timpson is a great place to work.

Customers' reward

Talent Spotting

You never know when you might find a great potential employee, they could be at a checkout or working behind the bar.

Always carry your business cards, so whenever you meet a sparky personality you can invite them to work for Timpson.

You gave me great service. If you ever think of working for Timpson, give me a call.

TIMPSON

Email:
greatplacetowork@timpson.com

Telephone:
0161 946 6200

AREA MANAGER

Calling card

In Reserve

Don't wait until you are short staffed before you start recruiting. Interview more people than you need and put a number of names on your waiting list.

Waiting list

Welcome Back

Over half the employees who leave us want to come back and most of them are welcome. Don't condemn people who have the courage to try opportunities elsewhere, the experience usually shows them Timpson is a great place to work. Welcome them back, they are often much better than when they left.

Ex employees

Everyone's Job

All of us should be on the look out for people who can strengthen our team. In addition, our 'Introduce a Friend Scheme' brings its own reward.

Everyone wears a recruiting hat

Instant Response

Every shop needs an application kit ready for potential recruits, it's so much better than asking them to contact Timpson house.

Forms at the ready

Reserve Strength

Recruitment should be discussed at every area meeting, even when you are fully staffed. A strong waiting list can often save an Area Manager from disaster.

Always on the table

Point of sale

Never stop recruiting. Always have a window bill to advertise job opportunities at Timpson.

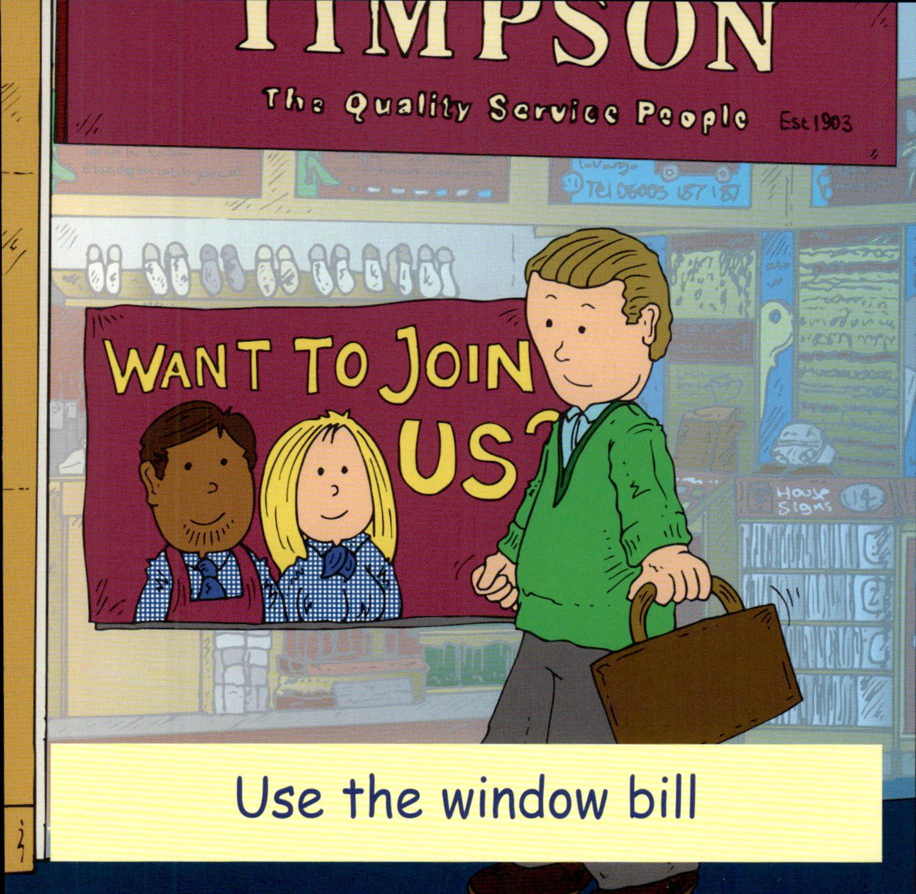

Use the window bill

Job Centre

Some of our star performers came to us through the Job Centre, but it's not the easiest way to recruit. Be prepared to wade through a few time wasters and drongos before finding the person you want.

The hard way

The last resort

Some firms always use advertising to find new staff, for us it's the last throw of the dice. It's expensive, takes time, and often brings disappointment.

TIMPSON

The Quality Service People

THE SUNDAY TIMES **100** BEST COMPANIES TO WORK FOR **2005**

Voted The Sunday Times *'Best Companies To Work For 2005'*

MANAGEMENT TRAINEES

Required **URGENTLY**

No experience necessary as full training given. Must be of smart appearance and have good communication skills. The successful applicant will be trained in key cutting, shoe repairs, engraving, watch repairs, retail management skills and above all first class customer service skills. Age no obstacle. Excellent promotion prospects.

Please Contact: The People Support Department

For an application pack call: **0161 946 6214**

Timpson Limited, Timpson House, Claverton Road, Wythenshawe, Manchester, M23 9TT.

Desperate measures

Never stop recruiting

Always look out for star quality, everyone you meet is a possible recruit. You never know when you are going to spot a super star.

You never know!

super star
Super Star

How to pick the best recruits

Have you ever wondered why some managers attract much better employees than others? The next few pages reveal their secret.

Make it fun

To attract the best people, create a great place to work. If your team enjoys coming to work, lots of people will want to join them.

Great place to work

Spread the word

Celebrate success in your window displays, feed fun news to the local newspaper and have a notice board in the shop that gives your customers all the news.

TIM TOP OF THE TIMPSON TREE

Congleton manager Tim Brown has won the customer care category in the Timpson nationwide annual awards. After receiving his trophy from Company Chairman John Timpson, Tim commented "I would just like to thank all my customers who bring so much to my shop every day."

Make the news

Desperate Measures

Never recruit the best of a bad bunch. If you can't find a candidate that matches your standards, you are better off with no one.

Don't recruit in desperation

Elite

Aim to become an exclusive club, the place where everyone wants to work, with all the best people fighting to win a job at Timpson.

Best of the best

Proper Preparation

Don't make an instant appointment, you and the recruit are making a long-term commitment, it shouldn't be rushed. Get to know each other before any decision is made.

Do not rush

Application Pack

Give the candidate plenty of information about the Company. We want them to understand our business before filling in the application form.

Provide an application pack

Real Life

Suggest their candidates visit their local shop to get first-hand experience of Timpson. Our staff should be only too happy to show them round,

The staff in this shop have the authority to do anything they feel will give their customers an amazing service.
John Timpson

Shop visit

Diary Date

Move quickly. Fix the time and place for your interview within a week of receiving the application form, don't keep potentially good candidates hanging around.

Set up interviews quickly

Open to all

You can't make a proper judgement from an application form, the only way to form a view is to meet. If possible, interview every candidate.

Interview every applicant

QUIET
INTERVIEW IN
PROGRESS

Interview techniques

Sensible Venue

Choose a place that is quiet, convenient and safe from any interruption. You can't carry out a proper interview in a car park or McDonalds.

Job Centre ✓
McDonalds ✗
Training Centre ✓
In The Car Park ✗
Choose right venue

Second Opinion

If possible, don't interview on your own, ask one of your area team or a shop manager to join you, it helps to have a second opinion.

Listening in

Study the form

Before meeting the candidate, study the application form carefully What does it tell you and indeed what does it not tell you. The form should provide plenty of hints to the right questions to ask.

WELL QUALIFIED
FLITS FROM JOB TO JOB
TIMPSON
Application Form
J. Smith
Married
Includes 7 GCSE's - 2 A Levels
Sept 1995 - Oct 1996 = McDonalds
Feb 1997 - Jan 1999 = TK Max
Jan - Mar 2004 = B&Q
August - Sept 2005 = British Gas
From Oct 2005 - present = Bank Clerk
Apprentice of the year 2005 British Gas
Captain Wrexham Albion FC 2005-2006
WHAT HAPPENED FOR 5 YEARS?
CLEARLY HAS SOME ABILITY
Read between the lines

Peer Pressure

If the candidate has visited one of our branches, talk to the team, they will have formed an impression which will probably be very accurate.

Talk to the team

Well turned out

You also are being interviewed. Your behaviour and appearance create the candidate's impression of Timpson. Look smart and be on time.

Look the part

No Interruptions

Don't let anything interrupt an interview, divert all calls and put a 'Do Not Disturb' sign on the interview room door.

Divert all calls

First Impressions

Within 30 seconds you will have formed an opinion. It's the simple things that count. Are they on time, do they look smart, have they the right attitude and do they really know about the job they are applying for?

Sorry I'm late!
PUNCTUALITY
DRESS
ATTITUDE
KNOWLEDGE
I thought you sold shoes!
Things to look for

Questions to get them talking

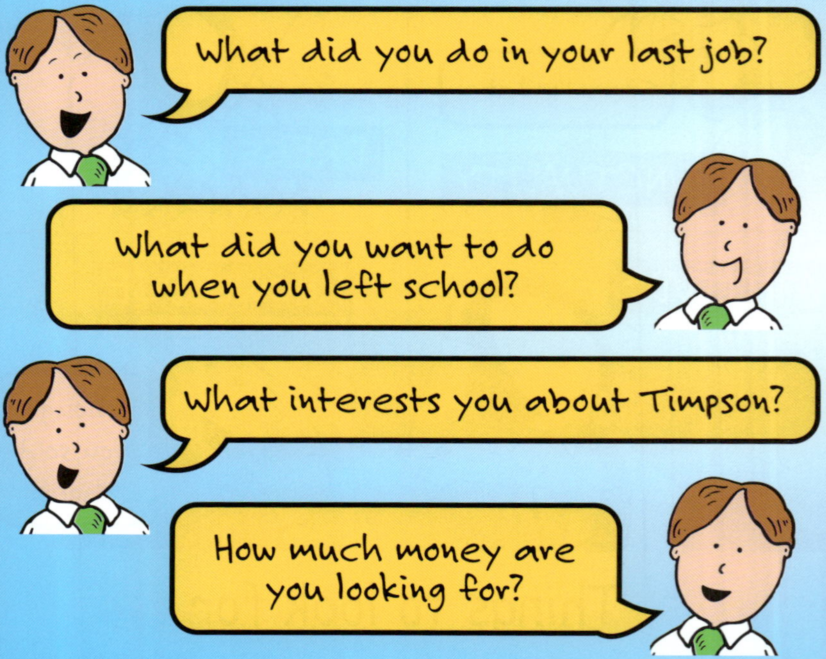

Why should we employ you?
When can you start?
What are your favourite hobbies?
Who is the best person you have worked for?

Boring Basics

Make sure you gather all the basic information. This check list covers everything you need to tell them and what they need to tell you.

INITIAL INTERVIEW

✓ or write N/A in box provided

1	Previous Employment	
2	Medical Record	
3	Criminal Record	
4	Driving License	
5	Type of Duties	
6	Hours of Work	
7	Shift Patterns	
8	Pay	
9	Manner of Payment (bank)	
10	Bank Details Required	

11	Holiday Payments	
12	Pension	
13	Sick Payments & Conditions	
14	Review Date	
15	Uniform	
16	Explain Application Form	
17	Explain Medical Form	
18	First Aid Certificate	
19	Fire Certificate	
20	Training	

Interviewers should record for reference the applicants:

APPEARANCE: ....

MANNER: ....

EXPERIENCE: ....

SUITABILITY: ....

EMPLOYMENT STATUE: ....

UNIFORM SIZE:..

SIGNATURE: ....

Check your facts

Some searching questions

Here are some questions that make you face up to reality. Think carefully and give yourself an honest answer.

Would you pay his/her wages with your own money?
Would you lend him/her £50?
Would he/she win Big Brother?

Be Blunt

While interviewing the candidate, write down anything relevant that comes into your mind. First impressions count and innermost thoughts really count.

Write everything down

Clear Direction

Towards the end of the interview, say what happens next. You don't make a decision at this stage, but tell them when and how you will be in contact.

Clarify the next steps

Invite Questions

Give every candidate a chance to raise topics of their choice. Is there anything else they want to say about themselves? Do they need to know more about the company? Their questions will tell you more about them.

Turn the tables

Friendly Farewell

Leave on good terms, with a smile and best wishes, whether you intend to offer a job or not, you want every candidate to leave feeling positive about Timpson.

Part on a positive note

Study the options

With every candidate you have to decide 'yes,' 'no' or 'maybe'. Don't make a snap judgement, although first impressions are generally best, it's good to leave the decision overnight, if you still feel the same in the morning, it's unlikely you will ever change your mind, so turn your instinct into action.

Decision time

Quick Response

Tell every candidate the result of their interview as soon as possible. Speak to the successful candidates first, if they turn down your offer, you will probably want to recruit your first reserve.

Don't keep them in suspense

TIMPSON

The Quality Service People

APPRENTICE / NEW STARTER MANUAL

2007

Apprentice training

Good Grounding

Our Apprentice Scheme can turn raw recruits into potential super stars within six months. We could be creating a loyal employee that stays for over 35 years.

Creating superstars

Sympathetic Ears

Place your new recruit with the right apprentice trainer. A good social fit makes a big difference to the recruit's learning process.

The right trainer

First day greeting

The person who carried out the interview should be one of the first to welcome a newcomer. If possible the Area Manager should speak to the starter on his first day and if possible, go to the shop and meet them in person.

Warm welcome

Relaxed Review

Within the first three weeks, take your apprentice for a chat over coffee, within 15 minutes you should discover all you need to know about their progress.

Informal questioning

No Bullying

We expect every employee to warmly welcome each new recruit. Come down hard on anyone who gives a new starter a rough time. Unpleasantness and initiation pranks are unacceptable.

No pranks

Be on line

Give your new starter your telephone number to use if they have a problem. Encourage them to ring at any time. Most won't, but all will appreciate that help is at hand.

AREA HELPLINE

07727 413889

Any problems, any time!

Always available

Under Review

Watch the progress of all your new starters, some learn a lot quicker than others. Within weeks they reveal their true character, ensure you make the most of their talents.

Talent spotting

Praise

Look out for signs of success and whenever possible, say "Well Done," in a tangible way.

Say well done

Call Home

With young starters who live at home, try to touch base with Mum or Dad and give a progress report, they will appreciate an honest opinion.

Progress report

No Hopers

Don't waste time on poor performers who have no intention of giving you their best shot. Dismiss them as soon as possible.

Dump the drongos!

How to teach an old dog new tricks
IMPSO

Career development

Everyone with potential must have the opportunity to learn. Training isn't just for apprentices. Great Timpson personalities still want to learn new skills right up to retirement.

Individual Tuition

We don't clone people. Our employees have a variety of attributes, and develop at different speeds. Our job is to help each individual reach their potential.

Develop the individual

Personal Responsibility

Timpson "Upside-down Management," makes people responsible for their own training, the training team is there to help them achieve their objectives, no one is forced to attend training courses, but most Timpson people like learning new skills.

Learn more skills

Career Training

Our training aims to help everyone develop their career and maximise their pay. We fill every field management role by promoting from within.

Sky's the limit

Self Motivation

We like ambitious people and expect everyone to have a goal – THE NEXT TWO PAGES WILL HELP INDIVIDUALS SET THEIR PERSONAL OBJECTIVES.

Personal ambition

My plan

SKILL LEVELS

	NOW	T/Y	EVENTUALLY
SHOE REPAIRS			
KEY CUTTING			
WATCH REPAIRS			
ENGRAVING			
HEALTH & SAFETY			
MANAGEMENT			
CUSTOMER CARE			

ROLE

JOB NOW	
JOB IN 2 YEARS	
EVENTUAL GOAL	

Personal objectives

MY PERSONAL AMBITIONS

E.G.

Buy a car
Buy a house
Visit Australia
Go to the Olympics
Live at number 10

MY TRAINING PLAN

- IBT's to visit
- Training course to attend
- Manuals to read

Progress Report

Everyone likes to know where they stand, provide them with a regular progress report.

Let people know how they're doing

Your Say

We encourage regular conversations, but some people feel they don't have the opportunity to talk about their progress. The 'Your Say' scheme gives everyone the right to talk and for their boss to listen.

The right to talk

Helping Hand

There are many ways we can help individuals improve their management and technical skills. Manuals, training days and in branch trainers all help individuals reach new skill levels.

TIMPSON
GUIDE TO KEY CUTTING
TIMPSON
GUIDE TO ENGRAVING
MANAGER
TIMPSON
GUIDE TO EXPERT SHOE REPAIRS
MANUALS
IN-BRANCH TRAINERS
TRAINING DAYS
SKILL ASSESSMENTS
Advanced Key Cutting
Expert
Help is at hand

A step up

Picking people for promotion is one of the toughest decisions. Get it right and you will see a dramatic improvement in the business, the wrong decision can create a whole new set of problems.

Promotion

Don't be frightened of high flyers

Jealousy and fear make some bosses stand in the way of future superstars. Your reputation will be enhanced if you train an Area Manager of the future.

Career blockers

Open Field

Every job must be widely advertised with a proper interview process.

Advertise properly

Warts an all

Candidates for promotion must know what they are letting themselves in for. It's easier to see the benefits than the pitfalls.

AREA MANAGER JOB DESCRIPTION

6.00 am starts	Pestered on the phone	Lots of travel
Nights away	Unpopular with partner	Best job in Timpson!

Crystal clear description

Makes you think

If you answer yes to all three questions on the opposite page, you have a candidate equipped for the job.

Vital questions

Testing

Have a probationary period for every new appointment. You and your employee will learn an awful lot in three months.

Have a trial period

In the deep end

The best experience comes through making mistakes but people need a boss who helps them through the learning process.

TIMPSON
The Quality Service People
THE AREA MANAGER'S GUIDE
CHAIRMANS VISIT
REFITS
SKILL TESTS
SICKNESS
HEALTH & SAFETY
TRAINING
WEEKLY FIGURES
RECRUITMENT
AREA REVIEW
STOCKTAKING
STORE CHECKERS
LODGE REPORT
APPRENTICES
CUSTOMER COMPLAINTS
AREA DINNER
NEW KEY BOARD
NEW BRANCH
MANUALS
Management Course
DAY OUT WITH EXPERIENCED AM
Provide the training

Keep in touch

Keep close contact with anyone in a new job. Have a detailed discussion every week and put the important points in writing.

Weekly feedback

Decision Time

At the end of the review period, make a decision and don't fudge it. Once the new manager has been confirmed in the job, there is no turning back.

Yes
No
TIMPSON

Super Star
TIMPSON

REMEMBER

Your business is as good as the people
who look after your customers!